Paleo & Specific Carbohydrate Diet for Ulcerative Colitis & Crohn's Disease

Easy Paleo and Specific Carbohydrate Cookbook featuring Delicious family-style recipes

EMANUEL D'SOUSA

ISBN 978-1-7771795-1-9

Table of Contents

What is Paleo Diet 1
  What to Eat 3
  What Not To Eat 3
  The Origin 4
  Why the Paleo Diet 5
  Why Specific Carbohydrate Diet...5
  #1 Have a friend join you 6
  #2 Prepare yourself properly..6
  #3 Set a goal..7
  #4 Stay faithful to your diet!...7
  #5 Record you're eating habits..8
  #6 Get enough sleep and move around 8
  #7 Track your progress...9
Myths about the Paleo Diet....................................**10**
  The paleo diet is a completely a carnivorous diet 10
  The paleo diet is not sustainable and is expensive............10
  The paleo is a low carbohydrate-diet 11
  The paleo diet is less suitable for women and more
  suitable for men...11
  You are likely to live up to thirty only 11
  The paleo is based on a fantasy 12
Benefits of the Paleo Diet....................................**13**
Do's and don'ts **17**
  Foods you can eat...17
  Foods you cannot eat 18
Grocery list...**19**
  Fats and Oils..21
  Flours 21
Paleo recipes...**24**
  1. Vegetable Frittata..24
  2. Primal Blueberry Waffles 26
  3. Pink & Delicious Pancakes 28

4. Scramble Eggs à la Provençale 30

5. Applesauce Seasoned Paleo Pancakes 32

6. Caveman Breakfast Hash.....................................34

7. Paleo Classic Apple and Spice Muffins 37

8. Healthy Granola Bars 39

9. Paleo Beef Jerky 41

10. Spicy Nuts 43

11. Watermelon & Kiwi with Fresh Herbs 44

12. Ginger Green Smoothie.....................................45

13. Salmon, Spinach & Apple Salad............................46

14. Sautéed Coconut Chicken 48

15. The Big Salad...50

16. Paleo Pizza 52

17. Macadamia Hummus with Vegetables 54

18. Carrot Soup 56

19. Piri Piri Chicken 58

20. Nutty Tilapia Fillets..60

21. Tandoori Chicken Drumsticks & Mango Chutney...62

22. Stuffed Sea Bass...64

23. Paleo Sausage Delight......................................66

24. Roasted Beef with Nutty Vegetables 68

25. Pork Chops with Apple 70

26. Tilapia with Thai Curry 71

27. Paleo Orange Chicken 73

28. Beef Goulash 75

29. Baked Beef with Vegetables 77

30. Quick Chocolate Bonbon 79

31. Cherry and Almond Butter Milkshake 81

32. Ginger Brownies 82

33. Banana with Coconut & Almond Butter................84

34. Coconut Whipped Cream 85

35. Paleo Pumpkin Muffins 86

36. Cauliflower Bites with Chili 88

37. Almond Flour Waffles......................................90

38. Peanut Butter Cookies 92

39. SCD Beef Burritos 94

40. Legal French Toast 96

41. Roasted Tomatoes 97

42. Specific Carbohydrate Diet Guacamole...................99

43. Pulled Hawaiian Pork..101

44. Paleo Shrimp Scampi..102

45. Eggs Baked in Avocado 104

46. Awesome Blossom Cauliflower............................105

47. Banana Muffins..106

48. Bacon-Wrapped Steak with Onions and Mushrooms
....108

49. Calming Coconut Smoothie 109

50. Anti-Inflammatory Smoothie................................110

51. Berry Anti-Inflammatory Smoothie 111

52. Beets'n'Nuts Smoothie..112

53. Cauliflangonut Smoothie 113

54. Red and White Smoothie.......................................114

55. Cauliflower Power Smoothie 115

Paleo Smoothies for Post-workout Support 116

56. Grapes of Watermelon Smoothie 117

57. Blueberry Pear Smoothie.......................................118

58. RePEARer Smoothie..119

59. Asparagus Smoothie 120

60. Blueberry Smoothie...121

Conclusion...122

What is Paleo Diet

Paleo Diet has been around for thousands of years. It is based on the diet of the Paleolithic man or the caveman, hence its name. It consists mainly of fish, meat, fruit, and vegetables. However, grains, dairy, legumes, and processed food are prohibited.

Specific Carbohydrate Diet is a diet designed specifically for Crohn's disease, Ulcerative Colitis, IBD, and IBS. While a popular diet for these targeted diseases, it has many incredible benefits for anyone wishing to have a healthy and well- balanced life. With a track record of helping thousands of individuals suffering from some form of bowel disease, the foods that are eaten within this diet are known to boost your quality of life.

The allowed foods are mainly those that early man ate before the development of agriculture. This diet's central core is predominantly one of meat, fish, eggs, vegetables, nuts, and low- sugar fruits. Adding elements such as starches and grains has led to a considerable increase in health problems ranging from severe bowel disorders to obesity and brain function disorders. It, therefore, makes sense to eat the diet as it was initially developed.

Since it is based on the Paleolithic diet, it is presumed that the meat you should consume should come from grass-fed, free-range animals. This diet existed way before industrialization; thus, it is based on natural, chemical-free food. Since modern-day living makes it challenging to achieve such criteria, you can choose food that comes closest.

Instead of buying canned berries, choose fresh berries instead. It is better if you can find organic fruits and vegetables. Farmer's markets usually offer fresh produce. Stick to whole, unprocessed foods instead of canned, preserved goods.

To make it easier for you to choose what to eat, refer to the list below:

What to Eat

Fruits

Vegetables

Seafood

Grass-fed Meat

 Healthy Fats

Nuts and Seeds

What Not To Eat

Grains

Dairy

Sugars

Processed Foods

Starches

Legumes

Alcohol

As a rule of thumb, stick to foods that are whole, raw, and unprocessed. Stay away from GMO food and processed food products. Always read the labels. If it contains more than three ingredients and you can't even read them, do not take it.

The Origin

The term "Paleo" is short for "Paleolithic," which refers to the idea of mimicking the food and diet lifestyle of our ancestors from over 10,000 years ago. Primarily, the diet revolves around only eating foods that cavemen could have consumed, before the days of agriculture.

So, how exactly are people on the Paleo Diet supposed to eat foods that require no farming? Any wild animal protein is permitted. Moreover, other sources such as wild fruits, vegetables, and nuts are all fair game in this diet. Surviving on these foods alone is indeed possible, as man has lasted on these for thousands of years.

Modern humans who embark on this diet are encouraged to buy as organically as possible since most of us cannot be hunters and gatherers and obtain food from lush forests and landscapes. Thus, it's important to replicate the caveman diet closely, avoiding pesticides, herbicides, and GMOs.

Although it is important to channel your inner caveman and adapt their diet plan, all aspects of the caveman lifestyle do not need to be implemented. For example, portion sizes for modern humans have significantly evolved. Cavemen had a more sporadic eating pattern, which may have included surviving on nuts and berries for a few days until they killed a big animal and were granted meat. Generally, you should still be eating three meals a day and normal-sized proportions.

In retrospect, our bodies seem to respond best to foods that were eaten before we began farming and maintaining livestock. Our bodies don't react well to processed and artificial foods that now make up most of the modern foods offered to us. The Paleo Diet works to cut out junk that has a negative effect on our bodies and instead provides all-natural and wholesome foods, with excellent health benefits.

Why the Paleo Diet

Starting any diet plan or changing your food routine in order to alter your lifestyle can be challenging. To gain the most from your experience on the Paleo Diet, it's essential to plan accordingly and know all the ins and outs of the diet. Staying motivated, encouraged, and educated throughout the process is not only recommended but required to succeed.

If you're an avid junk food eater or just the average American, switching to this diet will take some getting used to. The Paleo Diet consists of the healthiest, most organic, and wholesome foods. Thus, you'll not only maintain a lean figure but will have the ability to stay strong and energetic, with lasting health benefits.

Why Specific Carbohydrate Diet

The SCD is a gluten-free, grain-free, lactose-free, and refined sugar-free diet. Although this diet may seem similar to the no-carb diet, it does not entirely eliminate sweets and dairy. The carbs that are considered "short-chain carbohydrates" are what is allowed in this diet. Short-chain carbohydrates are fruit, honey, homemade yogurt, nuts, and legal vegetables.

Additionally, if you are looking to embark on this journey, it's essential to ask yourself why you want to do this. Having a concrete plan and a primary goal or objective will keep you on the right track. Especially for people will low will- power or a history of excessive weight gain, maintaining the correct mindset will prove beneficial in the long run.

It's normal for people to struggle with weight loss techniques and various diet plans when tasty temptations are everywhere we look. Particularly on this diet, where fried, cheesy, and delicious bread are to be avoided. Thus, there are several tips you can follow in order to stay on track and focused.

#1 Have a friend join you

Support systems are always encouraged on diet plans. Sticking to a limited number of foods can be tricky when attending events, parties, and other gatherings. Having a friend who is going through the same process will alleviate some of the stress for you and, in turn, make the task fun and an inclusive affair. Plus, you'll be able to exchange recipes, and maybe he/she is a phenomenal cook willing to share!

#2 Prepare yourself properly

You know your schedule and how likely you are to be

tempted, especially when you're hungry. It's essential to buy food in advance and even prepare it early if you know you won't have any time later. Being left with an empty stomach or no time will lead to bad food choices, and you'll stray from the diet. If you are headed to an event where you know there will be a lack of fresh Paleo food, try bringing your own snack or even a dish to share! Just because it's healthy doesn't mean people won't like it. Most people just opt for other unhealthy alternatives because they are fast, easy, and all-American favorites. A yummy guacamole dip or a meat and veggie dish will sure be a crowd-pleaser. You may even recruit prospective Paleo goers!

#3 Set a goal

When times get tough, you may want to resort to a cheat meal or indulge in something non-Paleo. To avoid this, it's essential to set a goal early on in the diet plan and stick with it. You need to assess whether this is a short-term process, or if you will be continuing the diet for an extended amount of time. It may also be useful to physically write down your goals for the diet and specific reasons to go Paleo. Put this list somewhere accessible and where you will be able to see it on a daily basis. Remind yourself that when working towards a goal, every single day counts!

#4 Stay faithful to your diet!

No matter who you are, temptation on diets is always prevalent. However, if you never take a quick bite of a snack in the first place, it will be easier to avoid it altogether. When you start cheating on your diet, you may be inclined to keep indulging in that snack. If you simply can't resist, however, take a small serving of it and walk away. For instance, a small piece of dark chocolate or a healthy non-Paleo food will do. If you find yourself completely off track for one day, start fresh the next morning. Don't deprive yourself and start your day with a killer Paleo breakfast.

#5 Record you're eating habits

If you are notorious for overeating, even on diets, it may be best to record the foods that you are consuming. Also though the Paleo diet contains all healthy foods, you should still be eating them in moderation. Frequently snacking in-between meals can really rack up the calories and can delay the weight loss process. If this is something you seem to struggle with or not, writing down everything you consume in a food diary will prove exciting and provide insight. This will increase your likelihood of succeeding and will help you reach your goal.

#6 Get enough sleep and move around

Getting an ample amount of sleep each night will ultimately improve your mood and will encourage weight loss. Sleep deprivation can often cause irritation and fatigue, which have you opting for unhealthy alternatives. Additionally, continually moving around and seeing progress from exercise will motivate you to continue your diet and put healthy foods into your body.

#7 Track your progress

Although not encouraged for everyone on this diet, frequent weigh-ins can be useful for some of you! Writing down daily progress reports or creating a chart can create a sort of game for you and ultimately prompt enthusiastic participation in this diet. Some people create small and significant goals and reward themselves when progress occurs.

Myths about the Paleo Diet

I have heard people make some bizarre comments about paleo and wondered where they were getting their ideas from. Maybe you have also come across some of these concepts. We must clarify some of these myths and misconceptions before we move on. Some of the common myths and misconceptions include:

The paleo diet is a completely a carnivorous diet

Yes, it is true that the paleo diet encourages that you eat grass-fed meat. However, this is not what the Paleo man ate alone. The paleo man ate wild fruits and vegetables. The paleo man did not get his nutrients only from meat.

The paleo diet is not sustainable and is expensive

While I know getting fresh vegetables and grass-fed meat in a world that embraces eating processed foods can be quite expensive, here is a question I want to pose to you; which one is more expensive: Keeping obesity at bay or treating those other cardiovascular diseases? You can choose to eat well and not have to worry about making too many visits to the doctor; the choice is yours.

The paleo is a low carbohydrate-diet

The idea of removing high starchy carbohydrates, especially grains that interfere with your insulin levels as well as your gut health is the best. Most people may regard the paleo diet as a low-carb diet since you will not be eating grains, which are usually high in carbohydrates. However, you don't have to go on a low-carb diet when on the paleo diet because you can still get your daily carbs from vegetables and fruits.

The paleo diet is less suitable for women and more suitable for men

While most men prefer meat for meals, most women would instead go for cakes, cookies, ice cream, and such. This, however, does not mean that a man is likely to benefit more from the diet. In any case, there are no specific paleo recipes for men and those for women. Furthermore, just because the men are the ones who went hunting and gathering during that period doesn't make it favorable to him alone. Of course, he used to hunt for his whole family.

You are likely to live up to thirty only

Cavemen indeed had a shorter lifespan. However, this has nothing to do with what he ate. Let us look at it from this point of view; those people then had very rough living conditions. Whenever there was a disease breakout, they did not have all the modern medicine that you do. They knew nothing about the existence of hospitals. That is why child mortality was very high then. Today, child mortality has gone down. I can only imagine how long the paleo man could live to if he ate the way he ate and had all the technological advancements we have today. I bet he would live for a very long time and not just thirty.

The paleo is based on a fantasy

Some people have this notion that adopting the paleo diet means that you fend for yourself by getting your hunting and gathering tools and going to the wild. This is, however, not the case. All you do in this diet is borrowing some lessons from their lifestyle. After all, they were our ancestors!

Now that we have cleared the misconceptions let us look at what you eat while on the Paleo diet.

Benefits of the Paleo Diet

Eating wholesome foods, vegetables, and fruits are promoted in the Paleo diet providing your body with the required minerals, salts, and vitamins. This has a positive effect on your health. Let us find out about the various benefits of the Paleo diet.

1.   Improves dental health

Acid-producing bacteria that cause damage to the teeth are reduced when this diet is followed. Vitamins A, D, and K help in the repair of tissue, while calcium helps in strengthening the bones and minimizing decay. Anti-inflammatory properties that can relieve symptoms of periodontal diseases are found in vitamin C.

2.   Reduces allergies

As allergens in your food are reduced, the allergies also go down. Eliminating dairy products and grains helps control allergies as eating anti-inflammatory foods helps to control the inflammation that leads to allergic responses.

3. Decreases inflammation

The high presence of anti-inflammatory properties in the Paleo diet decreases the risk of cardiovascular diseases, which can be caused due to inflammation.

4. Helps tackle diabetes

Lack of refined sugar, minimum fat intake promoted in this diet helps in keeping the sugar levels in check.

5. Helps in better sleep

As you cut down on chemicals and additives by following the Paleo diet, you will find that you feel naturally tired by night and feel the need to sleep. Serotonin, released by the brain, is not overridden by chemicals, and your body picks up the sleep signals better.

6. Helps in weight loss

The Paleo diet is naturally nutrient-dense and low in carbohydrates. Eliminating processed food will help you to lose weight.

7. Decreases risk of cancer

Scientific evidence shows that foods containing phytonutrients and antioxidants, as found in the Paleo diet, help fight diseases like cancer.

8. Strengthens hair

The nutrient density of the food consumed in the Paleo diet leads to improved thickness, strength, and shine of your hair. Zinc and iron, present in red meat and shellfish and biotin present in eggs are great for maintaining healthy hair and nails.

9. Keeps acne problems in control

A Paleo diet directly addresses the most common reasons for skin problems which are, inflammation, nutrient deficiencies, and gut dysbiosis. The excessive omega-6 fat present in refined oils causes inflammation. This is eliminated in the Paleo diet leading to a reduction of problems like acne, eczema, and psoriasis.

10. Increases energy levels

Refined foods are absorbed quickly, producing adrenal fatigue. With the Paleo diet, you eat foods with a low glycemic index. The sugars of such foods are absorbed slowly, hence a lag in energy is avoided, and you feel energetic throughout the day.

Let us share some of the recipes you can use while following the Paleo diet and help you reach your goal of a lean and healthy body.

Do's and don'ts

Foods you can eat

- Meats: Poultry, turkey, steak, bacon, ground beef, and pork are included in the diet. Look for grass-fed meats!

- Fish: Salmon, mackerel, trout, bass, sardines are preferred. Fish is protein-rich, and you should include more of it in your diet.

- Fresh seafood: You can feast on seafood and include crayfish, lobsters, crabs, clam, shrimps, and scallops in your meals

- Vegetables: Spinach, onions, tomatoes, carrots, cabbage, celery, sprouts, asparagus are all to be eaten. Vegetables like potatoes that contain high levels of starch are to be avoided.

- Fruits: Watermelons, blueberries, strawberries, apples, oranges, papaya, grapes, and lychees are fruits you can eat.

- Nuts: These should be consumed in moderate quantities only. Almonds, walnuts, macadamia nuts, pumpkin seeds, cashews, pine nuts, hazelnuts, and pecans can be included in your diet.

- Eggs: They are a good source of protein. In some diets, consumption of egg yolk is restricted but not in the Paleo diet.

- Oils: Olive oil, flaxseed oil, coconut oil, avocado oil, walnut oil, and macadamia oil are included in the diet to provide an energy source from natural fats and oils.

Foods you cannot eat

- All types of cereals

- Grains

- Legumes like peanut

- All dairy products

- Refined sugars

- Processed foods

- Potatoes

- Foods with high salt content

- Refined oils

Grocery list

- Condiments

- Capers in brine or oil

- Mustard

- Brown or Russian mustard

- Dijon or yellow mustard

- Grainy or English mustard

- Fish sauce

- Kalamata olives in brine or oil

- Mayonnaise, preferably homemade (to ensure that individual ingredients are all Paleo safe)

- Pesto, preferably homemade (to ensure that it remains dairy-free)

- Salt

- Kosher salt

- Pink Himalayan salt

- Sea salt

- Vinaigrettes, preferably homemade (to ensure that these do not contain sweeteners)

- Vinegar – almost all vinegar products are Paleo

safe, but there are a few manufacturers who try to pass off really cheap ones by adding food coloring and sugar. Read product labels before buying.

- Apple cider vinegar
- Balsamic vinegar
- Black currant vinegar
- Cane vinegar
- Coconut vinegar
- Date vinegar
- Jujube vinegar
- Kiwi fruit vinegar
- Malt vinegar
- Palm vinegar
- Persimmon vinegar
- Pomegranate vinegar
- Quince vinegar
- Raisin vinegar
- Raspberry vinegar
- Rice vinegar/rice wine vinegar/mirin
- Tomato vinegar
- Wolfberry vinegar

Fats and Oils

- Avocado oil (not suitable for cooking, but great for making vinaigrettes, and drizzling over meat and vegetables)

- Bacon drippings or bacon grease (from Paleo-safe bacon, store-bought or homemade)

- Clarified butter or ghee

- Coconut butter and coconut oil

- Duck fat (use as sparingly as possible)

- Flaxseed oil (same properties as avocado oil)

- Macadamia oil (same properties as avocado oil)

- Olive oil / extra virgin olive oil

Flours

Although there are Paleo-safe flours and starches, it would be best to use or consume these sparingly, especially if you are trying to lose weight, or if you are trying to control your blood sugar and insulin levels. Aside from almond flour/meal and coconut flour, (both are medium flours), you can also safely use:

- Light flours. These work well as binders and thickening agents and may be safely used as a cornstarch substitute. However, these cannot be

21

used to make baked goods (e.g., bread, pies, etc.) on their own. Light flours cannot hold their shape during prolonged cooking or baking and must be mixed with medium or dense flours. These include:

- Arrowroot powder

- Ground chia seeds

- Ground flaxseeds or flaxseed meal

- Kuzu starch

- Sweet potato starch (usually white-colored; not to be confused with sweet potato powder)

- Medium flours. These can be used as binders and thickening agents as well, but these can also be used in baking. These flours provide elasticity (bounce) to breads and can be successfully kneaded and proofed. These include:

- Chestnut flour

- Ground plantain and plantain flour (have distinct plantain flavor)

- Ground pumpkin

- Ground sweet potato

- Ground taro

- Ground winter squash

- Ground yucca

- Pumpkin seed flour

- Sweet potato powder (distinctly orange-colored, not to be confused with sweet potato starch)

- Tapioca flour/starch

- Dense flours. These should always be combined with light or medium flours when baking as these need excessive amounts of baking powder or baking soda to rise properly. These include:

- Cashew flour

- Hazelnut flour (has mild hazelnut flavor)

- Macadamia nut flour

- Pecan flour

- Sunflower seed flour

- Walnut flour

Paleo recipes

1.
Vegetable Frittata

Serves: 4

Prep Time: 15 minutes Cooking Time: 20 minutes

Ingredients

4 eggs

30 ml (2 tablespoons) olive oil

1 onion, chopped

1 garlic clove, minced

125 ml (½ cup) carrots, thinly sliced

125 ml (½ cup) red bell pepper, deseeded, julienne

1 zucchini, thinly sliced

125 ml (½ cup) baby spinach, chopped 15 ml (1 tablespoon) fresh basil, chopped

Sea salt and freshly ground pepper to taste

Fresh parsley, chopped for sprinkle

Directions:

1. In a bowl, whisk the eggs vigorously until fluffy, about 2 minutes.

2. Heat oil in a non-stick frying pan, sauté onions and garlic for 2-3 minutes on high heat until tender.

3. Lower the temperature to medium. Add red bell peppers, zucchini, spinach, and tomatoes. Cook for 5 minutes until vegetables are crisply tender. Add eggs and basil. Season with salt and pepper to taste. Cook for 10-15 minutes on medium-low heat until the eggs are done.

4. Cut into wedges, sprinkle with parsley, and serve hot.

Nutritional Information (per serving)

Calories: 258

Fat total: 22.1G, saturated fat: 6.5g Carbohydrates: 8.0g, dietary fiber: 2.6g Sugars: 3.8g, protein: 7.2G

2.
Primal Blueberry Waffles

Serves: 4

Prep Time: 15 minutes Cooking Time: 12-15 minutes

Ingredients:

250 ml (1 cup) blueberries

3 eggs, separated

250 ml (1 cup) almond flour 60 ml (¼ cup) almond milk 1 teaspoon vanilla extract

30 ml (2 tablespoons) olive oil

Maple syrup to sprinkle (optional – can be replaced by raw honey)

Directions:

1. Grease the waffle maker with olive oil or coconut butter, and pre-heat it.

2. In a mixing bowl, using an electric hand beater, whisk the egg whites on high speed until they form stiff peaks, about 2-3 minutes.

3. In another bowl, combine the egg yolks, the almond milk, and vanilla extract. Add the coconut flour and salt and olive oil. Mix well until you have a smooth batter.

4. Incorporate 1/3 of the egg whites into the batter, mixing well. Add another 1/3 of the egg whites and fold it in the batter until they are well incorporated. Repeat. You should have a light and fluffy batter.

5. Pour about 1/2 cup of the batter into the waffle maker, close the lid, and let it cook according to the manufacturer's instructions.

6. To serve, top each waffle with blueberries and drizzle with maple syrup or raw honey.

Nutritional Information (per serving)

Calories: 448

Fat total: 37.4g, saturated fat: 30.5g Carbohydrates: 24.3g, dietary fiber: 6.3g Sugars: 13.9g, Protein: 9.2G

3.
Pink & Delicious Pancakes

Serves: 4

Prep Time: 10 minutes Cooking Time: 10 minutes

Ingredients:

250 ml (1 cup) fresh raspberries

4 eggs

250 ml (1 cup) almond meal

125 ml (½ cup) unsweetened almond milk

1 teaspoon vanilla extract

10 ml (2 teaspoons) baking powder

2.5 ml (½ teaspoon) ground cinnamon 30 ml (2 tablespoons) coconut oil

30 ml (2 tablespoons) olive oil

Maple syrup for drizzle or fresh fruits with raw honey for garnish

Directions:

1. In a bowl, whisk together the raspberries and the eggs.

2. Mix in almond milk, olive oil, and vanilla extract

3. In another bowl, whisk together almond meal, baking powder, and cinnamon.

4. Gradually add the dry ingredients with the egg and blueberries. Combine well using a whisk.

5. Melt the coconut butter in a medium-sized frying pan on high heat. Spoon about 30 ml (2 tablespoons) of the batter into the pan. Cook for 2-3 minutes or until slightly golden on each side.

6. Drizzle with maple syrup or fresh fruits with raw honey for garnish and serve.

Nutritional Information (per serving)

Calories: 448

Fat total: 37.4g, saturated fat: 30.5g Carbohydrates: 24.3g, dietary fiber: 6.3g Sugars: 13.9G, Protein: 9.2G

4.
Scramble Eggs à la Provençale

Serves: 4

Prep Time: 5 minutes Cooking Time: 10 minutes

Ingredients:

125 ml (½ cup) onions, chopped

125 ml (½ cup) tomatoes, chopped

4 eggs

125 ml (½ cup) fresh basil leaves, chopped

2.5 ml (½ teaspoon) dried Provençale herb mix

Sea salt and freshly ground pepper to taste

30 ml (2 tablespoons) coconut oil

Directions:

1. In a mixing bowl, whisk the eggs until fluffy. Add Provençale herbs.

2. Melt the coconut oil in a medium frying pan, add onions, and sauté for 2-3 minutes until the onions are fragrant and tender. Add tomatoes and basil leaves. Season with salt and pepper.

3. Add eggs to the pan and cook for 3-5 minutes until the eggs are not runny anymore, occasionally

stirring to scramble the eggs.

4. Serve hot with paleo-approved breakfast sausages or bacon strips, if desired.

Nutritional Information (per serving – no bacon or sausage)

Calories: 251

Fat total: 22.4g, saturated fat: 14.5g Carbohydrates: 2.2G, dietary fiber: 0.5g Sugars: 1.7g, Protein: 11.5G

5.
Applesauce Seasoned Paleo Pancakes

Serves: 2

Prep Time: 10 minutes Cooking Time: 10 minutes

Ingredients

250 ml (1 cup) unsweetened applesauce, preferably homemade or organic

250 ml (1 cup) almond meal

3 eggs

60 ml (¼ cup) almond milk

2.5 ml (½ teaspoon) baking powder 5 ml (1 teaspoon) vanilla extract

1 ml (¼ teaspoon) ground nutmeg

1 ml (¼ teaspoon) ground cinnamon

30 ml (2 tablespoons) melted coconut oil

Olive oil for frying

Directions:

1. Beat eggs and applesauce together in a mixing bowl. Add vanilla, almond milk, olive oil.

2. Mix almond milk and vanilla extract with egg and potatoes.

3. In another bowl, mix almond meal, baking powder, ground nutmeg, and ground cinnamon.

4. Gradually add the dry ingredients to the egg mixture and combine well.

5. Heat about 1 tablespoon of olive oil in a medium frying non-stick pan. When the oil is hot, spoon about 60 ml (1/4 cup) of this batter into the pan and cook for 2-3 minutes on each side until slightly golden.

6. Serve the pancakes hot with a drizzle of organic maple syrup or fresh fruits with raw honey.

Nutritional Information (per serving)

Calories: 407

Fat total: 31.7g, saturated fat: 7.7g, Carbohydrates: 22.5G, dietary fiber: 7.9g

Sugars: 2.9g, Protein: 13.8g

6.
Caveman Breakfast Hash

Serves: 4

Prep Time: 15 minutes Cooking Time: 25 minutes

Ingredients:

For the sausage patties

450 g (1 pound) of ground pork or veal 1-2 garlic cloves, minced

2.5 ml (½ teaspoon) jalapeños, minced or 1 ml (¼ teaspoon) crushed hot chilies flakes

2.5 ml (½ teaspoon) dry thyme

2.5 ml (½ teaspoon) dry rosemary 1 ml (¼ teaspoon) fennel seeds

1 egg

Sea salt and freshly ground pepper to taste

For the hash (all ingredients to be chopped should be about the same size)

4 paleo-approved bacon strip, diced

4 breakfast sausages, homemade or paleo-approved, diced

4 eggs

1 tablespoon olive oil (optional) 1 yellow onion, diced

1 green bell pepper, diced 1 red bell pepper, diced

1 celery stalks, diced 1 sweet potato, diced 1 zucchini, diced

2 garlic cloves, minced

1 tablespoon jalapeños pepper, minced Sea salt and fresh ground pepper to taste

Directions:

Pre-heat the oven at 200°C/400 F.

For the sausage patties:

1. Place all the ingredients in a mixing bowl and combine well. Let rest and cover with a plastic wrap for at least 30 minutes. Form equal-sized patties.

2. In a large frying pan, heat some olive oil on high heat. Fry the patties until well done, about 3-4 minutes on each side on medium-high heat. Do not press down too much on the patties while cooking, or they will harden.

For the hash

1. In a large skillet, cook the bacon on high heat for 2-3 minutes until golden. Add onions and garlic, and continue cooking on medium heat for 2-3 minutes. Add sweet potatoes, cook for 5-6 minutes until the bacon is cooked. Add remaining ingredients. Cook for an additional 5-6 minutes or until all the

vegetables are tender-crisp. Season with salt and pepper to taste. Remove the pan from heat and reserve.

2. In another frying pan, cook the eggs sunny side up until done. Season with salt and pepper to taste

3. Spoon ¼ of the hash on a plate, top with one sunny egg. Repeat for each serving.

Nutritional Information (per serving)

Calories: 444

Fat total: 40.1G, saturated fat: 14.7g Carbohydrates: 13.3g, dietary fiber: 5.6g Sugars: 4.1G, Protein: 14.2G

7.
Paleo Classic Apple and Spice Muffins

Serves: 6

Prep time: 15 minutes Cooking time:

Ingredients:

1 cups almond flour

2 teaspoons baking powder

3 apples, peeled and shredded 2 tablespoons maple syrup

¾ cup coconut milk 2 large eggs

2 tablespoons coconut oil 1 teaspoon cinnamon

1/8 teaspoon nutmeg Vegetable cooking spray

Directions:

1. Preheat your oven to 180°C/350°F. Grease muffin tin with cooking spray.

2. In a bowl, mix dry ingredients well.

3. In another bowl, mix all wet ingredients until well combined. Add the mixture to the dry ingredients and whisk well.

4. Add the minced apple to the batter and mix well. Pour the batter into each the muffin hole until they are 3/4 full.

5. Bake for around 18-20 minutes until cooked thoroughly. You can check by inserting a toothpick in the middle of one of the muffins. Yields 12 muffins

Nutrition Information per muffin:

Calories: 168

Carbs: 17 g; Fat: 5.5 g Protein: 3 g Sugars: 16.3g

8.
Healthy Granola Bars

Serves: 2

Prep Time: 5 minutes Cooking Time: 15 minutes
Refrigerating time: 1-hour

Ingredients:

30 ml (2 tablespoons) pumpkin seeds

30 ml (2 tablespoons) poppy seeds

30 ml (2 tablespoons) sunflower seeds

30 ml (2 tablespoons) sesame seeds

30 ml (2 tablespoons) almonds, sliced

60 ml (4 tablespoons) freshly squeezed orange juice

15 ml (1 tablespoon) coconut oil

30 ml (2 tablespoons) raw honey

Directions:

1. Preheat oven to 180°C/350°F. Lightly grease a baking dish with olive oil.

2. Combine all ingredients in a bowl and seasons with salt and pepper.

3. Spread batter over a baking dish.

4. Bake for 10 to 15 minutes or until golden browned. Remove from the oven and let it cool.

5. Cut into bars and refrigerate for at least 1 hour until set before serving.

Nutritional Information (per serving)

Calories: 333

Fat total: 23.6g, saturated fat: 8.1G, Carbohydrates: 28.1G, dietary fiber: 3.4g Sugars: 30.5g, protein: 7.4g

9.
Paleo Beef Jerky

Serves: 2

Prep Time: 10 minutes

Marinating Time: 2 hours or overnight Cooking Time: 4 hours

Ingredients:

225 g (½ pound) flank steak

30 ml (2 tablespoons) Coconut Amino 1 garlic clove, mined

2.5 ml (½ teaspoon) smoked paprika

2.5 ml (½ teaspoon) chipotle powder

2.5 ml (½ teaspoon) onion powder

2.5 ml (½ teaspoon) ginger powder

2.5 ml (½ teaspoon) salt

2.5 ml (½ teaspoon) black pepper

Directions:

1. Preheat the oven to 60ºC/170°F. Lightly grease a baking dish.
2. Combine all ingredients in a bowl and mix.

3. Leave marinated for at least 2 hours or overnight.

4. Put the steak on the baking dish and bake for 3 to 4 hours.

Nutritional Information (per serving)

Calories: 234

Fat total: 9.6g, saturated fat: 3.9g Carbohydrates: 3.1g, dietary fiber: 0.5g Sugars: 0.0g, protein: 31.9G

10.
Spicy Nuts

Serves: 2

Prep Time: 5 minutes Cooking Time: 0 minutes

Ingredients:

5 ml (1 teaspoon) coconut oil 60 ml (¼ cup) pecans, toasted

60 ml (¼ cup) almonds, toasted 60 ml (¼ cup) walnuts, toasted

2.5 ml (½ teaspoon) chili powder 1 ml (¼ teaspoon) cumin

Pinch of salt and pepper

Directions:

1. Toss all ingredients in a mixing bowl and season with salt and pepper.

Nutritional Information (per serving)

Calories: 281

Fat total: 27.2G, saturated fat: 3.8g Carbohydrates: 6.5g, dietary fiber: 4.1G Sugars: 1.2G, protein: 7.7g

11.
Watermelon & Kiwi with Fresh Herbs

Serves: 2

Prep Time: 10 minutes Cooking Time: 0 minutes

Ingredients:

1000 ml (4 cups) watermelon

1 kiwi, chopped

2.5 ml (½ teaspoon) fresh oregano, chopped

2.5 ml (½ teaspoon) fresh cilantro, chopped

2.5 ml (½ teaspoon) fresh mint leaves

2.5 ml (½ teaspoon) fresh basil leaves, chopped

2.5 ml (½ teaspoon) fresh parsley, chopped

0.5 ml (⅛ teaspoon) salt Pinch of ground black pepper

Directions:

1. Toss all ingredients in a mixing bowl and season with salt and pepper.

Nutritional Information (per serving)

Calories: 116

Fat total: 0.7g, saturated fat: 0.0g Carbohydrates: 28.9g, dietary fiber: 2.6g Sugars: 22.3G, protein: 2.4g

12.
Ginger Green Smoothie

Serves: 1

Prep Time: 10 minutes Cooking Time: 0 minutes

Ingredients:

1 cup of frozen mango pieces

1 apple, peeled, and core removed

¼ teaspoon, fresh ginger

30 ml (2 tablespoons) flax seeds

1 kale leave

60 ml (¼ cup) spinach

15 ml (1 tablespoon) lemon juice

250 ml (1 cup) water

Directions:

1. Place all the ingredients in blender or juicer and pulse until smooth.
2. Serve and enjoy!

Nutritional Information (per serving)

Calories: 163

Fat total: 2.4g, saturated fat: 0.0g Carbohydrates: 31.6g, dietary fiber: 8.8g Sugars: 17.3g, protein: 4.9g

13.
Salmon, Spinach & Apple Salad

Serves: 2

Prep Time: 15 minutes Cooking Time: 30 minutes

Ingredients:

225 g (½ pound) salmon fillets

For salad

250 ml (1 cup) baby spinach 125 ml (½ cup) lettuce

125 ml (½ cup) cabbage, shredded

1 tart apple such as Granny Smith, sliced

For dressing

30 ml (2 tablespoons) olive oil

30 ml (2 tablespoons) apple cider vinegar

1 large shallot, minced

Salt and black pepper, to taste

Directions:

1. Preheat the oven to 180°C/350° F.

2. Place salmon fillet on a baking dish. Season with salt and pepper.

3. Add some water to cover fish. Cover with foil.

4. Bake for 10 minutes. Remove from the oven and set aside.

5. In a large bowl, add salad ingredients and mix.

6. In another bowl, add all dressing ingredients and whisk till well combined.

7. Pour dressing over salad and toss to coat.

8. Serve salad with baked fish fillets.

Nutritional Information (per serving)

Calories: 334

Fat total: 30.1G, saturated fat: 3.0g Carbohydrates: 15.6g, dietary fiber: 3.1G Sugars: 10.4g, protein: 22.9g

14.
Sautéed Coconut Chicken

Serves: 3-4

Prep Time: 10 minutes Cooking Time: 20 minutes

Ingredients:

450 g (1 pound) boneless and skinless chicken breasts cut in strips

60 ml (¼ cup) coconut flour

60 ml (¼ cup) shredded coconut, organic, unsweetened

0.5 ml (⅛ teaspoon) sea salt 1 egg

30 ml (2 tablespoons) coconut oil

Directions:

1. Whisk together coconut flour, shredded coconut, and salt in a medium bowl.

2. In another bowl, beat egg.

3. Dip chicken breasts strips in the egg and then into the flour mixture.

4. Heat oil in a frying pan over medium-high heat.

5. Place chicken in the pan and cook until golden brown from both sides.

6. Remove from the pan and serve on a plate.

Nutritional Information (per serving)

Calories: 298

Fat total: 15.1G, saturated fat: 10.6g Carbohydrates: 6.5g, dietary fiber: 3.9g Sugars: 1.2G, protein: 34.3g

15.
The Big Salad

Serves: 4

Prep Time: 20 minutes Cooking Time: 0 minute

Ingredients

For Salad

300 grams (2 cups) cooked chicken breast, chopped

2 liters (8 cups) spring mix lettuce 1 English cucumber, diced

12 cherry tomatoes

1 avocado, diced

60 ml (¼ cup) dry unsweetened cranberries

60 ml (¼ cup) chopped raw pecans or any favorite nuts

Sea salt and freshly ground pepper to taste

For Dressing – yield approximately 425 ml (1⅔cup)

1 cup extra virgin, cold press olive oil 60 ml (¼ cup) red wine vinegar 15 ml (1 tablespoon) Dijon mustard

30 ml (2 tablespoons) raw honey 60 ml (¼ cup) fresh basil leaves

Directions:

1. Blend together until smooth all the ingredient of the dressing

2. In a large salad bowl, place all the salad ingredients, season with salt and pepper to taste, add some dressing to taste, and mix well.

Nutritional Information (per serving)

Calories: 398

Fat total: 15.1G, saturated fat: 10.6g Carbohydrates: 6.5g, dietary fiber: 3.9g Sugars: 1.2G, protein: 34.3g

16.
Paleo Pizza

Serves: 8

Prep Time: 10 minutes Cooking Time: 55 minutes

Ingredients

For crust:

1000 ml (4 cups) almond flour

2 eggs

45 ml (3 tablespoons) olive oil

5 ml (1 teaspoon) garlic powder 1 ml (¼ teaspoon) baking soda

2.5 ml (1½ tablespoon) fresh rosemary, chopped

For toppings:

250 ml (1 cup) organic marinara sauce

485 g (1 pound) Italian paleo pork sausage, sliced

250 ml (1 cup) yellow summer squash, diced

3 scallions, chopped

15 ml (1 tablespoon) basil leaves 2 small tomatoes, diced 125 ml (½ cup) roasted red peppers, diced

15 ml (1 tablespoon) black olives, sliced Salt to taste

Directions:

1. Preheat the oven to 180°C/350° F. Lightly grease a pizza pan.

2. Place all the crust ingredients in a food processor and pulse until a dough forms.

3. Form a ball with the dough using your hands. Place the ball in the center of a greased pizza pan. Then press the dough using your hands, patting and shaping it into a circle. Bake for 20 minutes or until cooked. Remove from the oven. Let it cool.

4. In a bowl, add sausages, squash, scallions, basil, tomatoes, red pepper, olives, and salt and mix till well combined.

5. Spread pizza base with marinara sauce. Top with sausage mixture.

6. Return to oven and bake again for 25 to 35 minutes or until the top is lightly golden.

Nutritional Information (per serving)

Calories: 433

Fat total: 35.3g, saturated fat: 7.5g Carbohydrates: 12.9g, dietary fiber: 4.9g Sugars: 5.1G, protein: 18.7g

17.
Macadamia Hummus with Vegetables

Serves: 4

Prep Time: 20 minutes Refrigerating Time: 30-45 minutes

Ingredients:

750 ml (3 cups) macadamia nuts

60 ml (¼ cup) freshly squeezed lemon juice

60 ml (¼ cup) olive oil 2 garlic cloves, minced

2.5 ml (½ teaspoon) salt 125 ml (½ cup) water

500 ml (2 cups) of baby carrots

1 English cucumber, chopped into sticks 1 Sweet pepper, deseeded and sliced

Directions:

1. Place all the ingredients in a food processor except carrots and cucumbers and blend until smooth and thick.

2. Place hummus in a bowl and refrigerate to chill for 30 to 45 minutes before serving. Will keep for up to a week in the refrigerator.

3. Serve with the cut vegetables.

Nutritional Information (per serving)

Calories: 419

Fat total: 40.7g, saturated fat: 6.5g Carbohydrates: 15.7G, dietary fiber: 6.0g Sugars: 3.9g, protein: 5.3g

18.
Carrot Soup

Serves: 2

Prep Time: 15 minutes Cooking Time: 30 minutes

Ingredients:

30 ml (2 tablespoons) coconut oil

2 bay leaves

1 onion, sliced

4 garlic cloves, minced

250 ml (1 cup) carrots, chopped

2 turnips, chopped

2 sweet potatoes, cubed

1 ml (¼ teaspoon) dried thyme 1000 ml (4 cups) chicken broth

30 ml (2 tablespoons) fresh chives, chopped

Sea salt and freshly ground pepper to taste

Directions:

1. Heat oil in a large soup pan.

2. Stir in bay leaves, onion, and garlic, and sauté for few minutes until fragrant and tender.

3. Add carrots, turnips, sweet potatoes, and dried

thyme, and continue to cook until the vegetables are tender.

4. Add broth and bring to boil. Cover and cook for 15 to 20 minutes.

5. Discard bay leaves. Pour soup in a food processor and pulse until smooth.

6. Season with salt and pepper.

7. Return to soup pan and let it simmer for 5 minutes.

8. Put soup in a bowl, sprinkle with chives, and serve hot.

Nutritional Information (per serving)

Calories: 340

Fat total: 15.5g, saturated fat: 12.2G Carbohydrates: 43.7g, dietary fiber: 8.5g Sugars: 11.0g, protein: 8.7g

19.
Piri Piri Chicken

Serves: 4

Prep Time: 30 minutes Cooking Time: 65 minutes

Marinade time: 4h00 up to 12H00

Ingredients:

1 whole organic chicken

1 tablespoon of Piri Piri spice mix 4 garlic cloves, minced

1 onion

60 ml (¼ cup) freshly squeezed lemon juice

60 ml (¼cup) organic maple syrup 5 ml (1 teaspoon) sea salt

85 ml (⅓ cup) olive oil

30 ml (2 tablespoons) apple cider vinegar

Sea salt and fresh ground pepper to taste

Directions:

1. Mix all the ingredients except the chickens in a food processor. Blend until you obtain a smooth marinade.

2. Place the chicken on a working surface, breast side

down. With a large and sharp knife, cut open the back of the chicken so that it will flatten and open up. Turn the chicken over, and press firmly to flatten. Repeat for the second chicken.

3. In a large zip lock bag, place one chicken in with half of the marinade. Repeat with the second chicken. Refrigerate for a minimum of 4 hours and up to 12 hours.

4. Remove both chickens from the marinade, and place in a roasting oven pan. Place the chickens, breast side facing up. Season with salt and pepper to taste. Reserve the marinade.

5. Place the excess marinade in a small saucepan, and cook on low heat for 20 minutes

6. Place the chickens on the middle rack, in pre-heated 400°F oven, and cook for 30 minutes.

7. After 30 minutes, take out the chicken, smear with some of the marinade on both sides, and cook for another 30 minutes.

8. Brush the breast side with the rest of the marinade, and broil for 5 minutes.

9. Cut the chicken in pieces, and serve with steamed vegetables of your choice.

Nutritional Information (per serving)

Calories: 444

Fat total: 40.1G, saturated fat: 14.7g Carbohydrates: 13.3g, dietary fiber: 5.6g Sugars: 4.1G, protein: 14.2G

20.
Nutty Tilapia Fillets

Serves: 4

Prep Time: 15 minutes Cooking Time: 10 minutes

Ingredients:

4 large Tilapia fillets

15 ml (1 tablespoon) black peppercorn 8 ml (½ tablespoon) fennel seeds

8 ml (½ tablespoon) smoked paprika

45 ml (3 tablespoons) coconut butter or grass-fed butter

125 ml (½ cup) of pecan

15 ml (1 tablespoon) fresh chopped flat leave parsley

Sea salt & fresh ground pepper to taste 1 lemon, sliced

Directions:

1. Using a pestle and a mortar, crush and grind together peppercorn, fennel seeds, and paprika

2. Season both sides of the tilapia with the spices.

3. Using a frying pan, melt 2 tablespoons of the butter on medium heat. Add the fillets, and cook for 4 minutes, turn the tilapia over and cook for an

additional 3 to 4 minutes until the fish is done.

4. Place your cooked fillets on a warm serving plate and reserve.

5. In the same hot frying pan, add the rest of the butter and the pecans. Cook for about 1 minute. Add some lemon juice to taste, and mix well.

6. Place the lemony nuts on the fillets, sprinkle with the parsley, and serve with your favorite side vegetables and lemon slices.

Nutritional Information (per serving)

Calories: 444

Fat total: 40.1G, saturated fat: 14.7g Carbohydrates: 13.3g, dietary fiber: 5.6g Sugars: 4.1G, protein: 14.2G

21.
Tandoori Chicken Drumsticks & Mango Chutney

Serves: 8

Prep Time: 45 minutes Cooking Time: 30 minutes
Marinade time: 4 hours

Ingredients:

15 chicken drumsticks

Tandoori mix:

250 ml (1 cup) coconut milk Juice of 2 lemons

125 ml (½ cup) olive oil

60ml (¼ cup) tandoori spices

15 ml (1 tablespoon) red sweet paprika Sea salt & fresh
ground pepper to taste

Mango Chutney:

30 ml (2 tablespoons) olive oil 2 garlic cloves, minced

15 ml (1 tablespoon) minced fresh ginger 2 mangoes,
peeled and cubed

30 ml (2 tablespoons) raw honey 60 ml (¼ cup) white
vinegar

60 ml (¼ cup) water 2 cinnamon sticks

4 cloves

1-2 pinches of crushed chilies to taste Sea salt & fresh
ground pepper to taste

Directions:

1. Put all the ingredients for the tandoori mix together in a zip lock bag or a container, place the chicken in, and let marinate for at least 4h00.

2. For the chutney, in a small frying pan, heat the oil on high, reduce heat to medium, and cook the garlic and ginger for 2 to 3 minutes. Add all the remaining ingredients and cook covered for an additional 15 minutes on low heat. Remove the cover and cook another 10 minutes or until you obtain a consistent chutney. Cool before serving

3. Pre-heat oven to 400°F.

4. Place the drumsticks on a lightly oiled baking sheet. Cook for 30 minutes until the chicken is well cooked.

5. Serve with the mango chutney and your favorite steamed vegetables.

Nutritional Information (per serving)

Calories: 444

Fat total: 40.1G, saturated fat: 14.7g Carbohydrates: 13.3g, dietary fiber: 5.6 g Sugars: 4.1G, protein: 14.2G

22.
Stuffed Sea Bass

Serves: 4

Prep Time: 15 minutes Cooking Time: 25 minutes

Ingredients:

4 sea bass, about 350 to 450 grams (¾ to 1 pound) each, cleaned, head removed

125 ml (½ cup) olive oil

45 ml (3 tablespoons) olive oil

225 g (½ pound) white mushrooms, sliced

1 tablespoon fresh parsley, minced 1 green pepper, diced

Freshly squeezed lemon juice to taste Sea salt and fresh ground pepper to taste

Directions:

1. Pre-heat the oven at 305°C/425°F.

2. Salt and pepper the inside of the bass. Add lemon juice to taste.

3. Place each fish on a foil sheet large enough to cover the fish.

4. Melt half of the butter in a medium-size frying pan,

add the shallots and cook 2-3 minutes. Add the mushroom, pepper, and parsley. Season with salt and pepper to taste, and cook for an additional 6 minutes until vegetables are tender.

5. Stuff each fish with ¼ of the vegetable mix, and brush the fish with olive oil. Seal the aluminum foil well. Place the foil packets on a baking sheet. Cook for 16 minutes.

6. Take out of the oven and make sure the fish is well cooked. If not, bake for an additional 2 minutes or until cooked.

7. Serve with lemon slices and your favorite vegetables.

Nutritional Information (per serving)

Calories: 444

Fat total: 40.1G, saturated fat: 14.7g Carbohydrates: 13.3g, dietary fiber: 5.6g Sugars: 4.1G, protein: 14.2G

23.
Paleo Sausage Delight

Serves: 4

Prep Time: 15 minutes Cooking Time: 25 minutes

Ingredients:

6 Paleo-approved sausages of your choice

60 ml (¼ cup) olive oil

60 ml (¼ cup) apple cider vinegar 20 white mushrooms, trimmed

¼ cup fresh flat parsley, minced

2 sweet peppers, sliced in 1-inch strips 2 red onions, sliced in ½ inch strips

Sea salt and fresh ground pepper to taste

Directions:

1. Pre-heat the oven at 200°C/400°F.

2. In a large mixing bowl, combine all ingredients except parsley. Season with salt and freshly ground pepper to taste.

3. Lay the sausages and vegetable mix on a parchment paper-covered baking sheet and cook for 40 minutes.

4. Sprinkle with parsley and serve with your favorite mustard and a side of slaw.

Nutritional Information (per serving)

Calories: 444

Fat total: 40.1G, Saturated fat: 14.7g Carbohydrates: 13.3g, dietary fiber: 5.6g Sugars: 4.1G, protein: 14.2G

24.
Roasted Beef with Nutty Vegetables

Serves: 4

Prep Time: 15 minutes Cooking Time: 35 minutes

Ingredients:

30 ml (2 tablespoons) olive oil

450 g (2 pounds) lean beef steak (brisket), sliced

30 ml (2 tablespoons) grainy Dijon Mustard
Montreal steak spice to taste Garlic powder to taste

1 onion, sliced

15 ml (1 tablespoon) garlic, minced

250 ml (1 cup) asparagus, sliced

2 zucchinis, cubed

30 ml (2 tablespoons) almond butter

30 ml (2 tablespoons) almond slivers (optional)

Salt and pepper to taste

Directions:

1. Preheat the oven to 160°C/325°F.

2. Heat oil in a skillet on high heat.

3. Rub each steak with mustard, Montreal steak

spices, and garlic. When the skillet is hot, stir in the steak slices and cook for 1-2 minutes on each side until beef is nicely colored.

4. Transfer beef to a baking dish, season with salt and pepper. Place in preheated oven and bake for 10-15 minutes, depending on steak thickness and how you like your steak cooked. When the steaks are cooked to your liking, remove from oven and let rest for a few minutes before serving. This will make your steak juicier.

5. While steaks are baking, in the same skillet, add some more olive oil if necessary, sauté onions and almond slivers (optional) for 2-3 minutes, stirring often. Add asparagus and zucchini and cook 4-5 minutes until vegetables are tender but still crispy. Remove from heat, add almond butter and parsley. Reserve.

6. Serve each steak with a generous portion of the nutty vegetables.

Nutritional Information (per serving)

Calories: 449

Fat total: 29.0g, saturated fat: 7.8g Carbohydrates: 9.5g, Dietary fiber: 2.5g Sugars: 3.9g, protein: 37.5g

25.
Pork Chops with Apple

Serves: 2

Prep Time: 10 minutes Cooking Time: 20 minutes

Ingredients:

15 ml (1 tablespoon) coconut oil

2 pork chops

1 large onion, sliced 2 apples, sliced

Salt and freshly ground black pepper to taste

Directions:

1. Heat oil in a large pan.

2. Put chops in the pan, and cook for 5 minutes on each side until golden browned.

3. Add onion and apples and continue to cook for 7 to 9 minutes until the onion and apples are tender.

4. Sprinkle with salt and pepper and serve.

Nutritional Information (per serving)

Calories: 439

Fat total: 26.7g, saturated fat: 13.3g Carbohydrates: 31.9g, dietary fiber: 5.9g Sugars: 30.9g, protein: 18.7g

26.
Tilapia with Thai Curry

Serves: 2

Prep Time: 10 minutes Cooking Time: 25 minutes

Ingredients

125 ml (½ cup) coconut milk 250 ml (1 cup) fresh basil leaves

60 ml (4 tablespoons) Thai curry paste 30 ml (2 tablespoons) olive oil

2 tilapia fillets

1 large red bell peppers, deseeded, julienne

1 onion, sliced

60 ml (¼ cup) scallions, sliced 30 ml (2 tablespoons) fish sauce*

Salt and freshly ground black pepper to taste

Directions:

1. Place coconut milk, basil leaves, and Thai curry paste into the food processor and blend until smooth.

2. Heat oil in a large pan. Add tilapia fillets, and cook for 5 minutes on each side until little browned. Remove tilapia to a plate, and set aside.

3. Add red bell peppers, onion, and scallions in the same pan and cook until the vegetables are tender.

4. Add coconut milk mixture, and cook for 5 minutes until thickens. Add in reserved fish fillets; simmer until tilapia is heated through.

5. Drizzle fish sauce, season with salt and pepper, and serve.

Make sure that the fish sauce is entirely paleo, containing fish and salt only. It is suggested to read the label before purchasing.

Nutritional Information (per serving)

Calories: 441

Fat total: 29.7g, saturated fat: 15.1G Carbohydrates: 30.1G, dietary fiber: 4.7g Sugars: 10.6g, protein: 25.3G

27.
Paleo Orange Chicken

Serves: 2

Prep Time: 5 minutes Cooking Time: 20 minutes

Ingredients:

15 ml (1 tablespoon) coconut oil

225 g (½ pound) boneless chicken breast, cut into strips

1 garlic clove, minced

125 ml (½ cup) fresh orange juice 30 ml (2 tablespoons) grated orange Salt and pepper for seasoning

Directions:

1. Heat oil in a large frying pan over medium heat.

2. Stir in garlic and sauté 1 minute. Add chicken strips, and cook a few minutes, occasionally stirring until chicken is not pink anymore.

3. Add orange juice, cover, and continue to cook for 15 minutes over medium-low, until chicken is tender and juices almost run clear.

4. Sprinkle grated orange, season with salt and pepper, and serve.

Nutritional Information (per serving)

Calories: 310

Fat total: 15.3G, saturated fat: 8.2G Carbohydrates: 8.3g,
dietary fiber: 0.0g Sugars: 6.3g, protein: 33.5g

28.
Beef Goulash

Serves: 4

Prep Time: 20 minutes Cooking Time: 2h00

Ingredients:

1 kg (2 pounds) boneless stew beef such as chuck roast

30 ml (2 tablespoons) olive oil 1 large onion, chopped

4 garlic clove, minced

5 ml (1 teaspoon) caraway seeds

1 red bell pepper, deseeded, julienne 2 sweet potatoes, peeled and cubed 2 tomatoes, chopped

5 ml (1 teaspoon) salt

15 ml (1 tablespoon) jalapeños pepper, minced

500 ml (2 cups) beef broth Salt and pepper

Directions:

1. Cut beef into same size cube, about 4-5 cm (1-2 inches). Dry beef with a paper towel.

2. Heat oil in a large and deep skillet. Add beef and brown the meat very well, in batches if necessary. For proper browning, the beef cubes should not touch each other in the pan. Remove the meat from the skillet and reserve.

3. Add oil if necessary. Sauté onions for few minutes until translucent. Add in garlic, and cook for 2 minutes. Add the spices, mix well. Add red bell peppers and tomatoes and cook for 5 minutes. Add the reserved beef

4. Season with salt and pepper to taste, and add the jalapeños chili.

5. Add broth, and bring to a boil on high heat. Reduce heat to medium-low. Cover and cook for 1H00. Add sweet potatoes and cook for an additional 30 minutes. The meat should be very tender and easily cut with a fork. Taste and adjust seasoning with salt or pepper.

6. Serve hot with a side green salad.

Nutritional Information (per serving)

Calories: 269

Fat total: 23.7g, saturated fat: 7.5g Carbohydrates: 6.6g, dietary fiber: 1.6g Sugars: 3.3g, protein: 7.9g

29.
Baked Beef with Vegetables

Serves: 4

Prep Time: 10 minutes Marinating Time: 2 hours
Cooking Time: 35 minutes

Ingredients:

30 ml (2 tablespoons) coconut oil 225 g

(½ pound) boneless beef strips

1 small red onion, chopped

2 cloves garlic, chopped

125 ml (½ cup) carrots, sliced

1000 ml (4 cups) butternut squash, chopped

1 sweet potato, chopped

2.5 ml (½ teaspoon) dried thyme

2.5 ml (½ teaspoon) dried rosemary 60 ml (¼ cup)
coconut amino

2.5 ml (½ teaspoon) ground black pepper

Directions:

1. In a large bowl, add all ingredients except
   vegetables. Mix well. Let marinate for 30 minutes.

2. Preheat the oven to 180°C/350° F.

3. Toss in vegetables as well.

4. Place beef and vegetables in the baking dish, cover the dish completely with foil, and bake for 30 to 35 minutes. After that, remove foil and roast again for 10 minutes.

Nutritional Information (per serving)

Calories: 353

Fat total: 27.6G, saturated fat: 14.9g Carbohydrates: 17.8g, dietary fiber: 3.3g Sugars: 4.8g, protein: 9.8g

30.
Quick Chocolate Bonbon

Serves: 4-6

Prep Time: 20 minutes Cooking Time: 5-10 minutes
Freezing Time: 20 minutes

Ingredients:

125 ml (½ cup) dark chocolate chunks (70% or more cocoa)

250 ml (1 cup) raspberry, packed (fresh or frozen)

15 ml (1 tablespoon) of raw honey 5 ml (1 teaspoon) crushed almonds

Directions:

1. Melt chocolate over a double boiler. You can also microwave the chocolate until just melted.

2. Take a paintbrush and paint a mini cupcake mold or a candy mold with the chocolate. Paint thickly all around walls and base of the cups, remembering to keep a little melted chocolate for covering the candies.

3. Place in the freezer to set for 10 minutes.

4. In the meantime, puree the raspberry in a blender or food processor until smooth and strain it through a fine sieve to remove the seeds. Add the raw honey to the raspberry puree and mix well. Set aside

5. After 10 minutes, remove from the freezer. Equally, spoon the raspberry puree in all the chocolate molds. Sprinkle with crushed almonds. Paint the top with the melted chocolate to cover the bonbons.

6. Place in the freezer again to harden for 10 minutes.

7. Lastly, pop the candies out of the mold into a plate, keeping upside down and serve.

Nutritional Information (per serving)

Calories: 238

Fat total: 13.0g, saturated fat: 8.8g Carbohydrates: 27.1G, dietary fiber: 2.1G Sugars: 22.7G, protein: 3.6g

31.
Cherry and Almond Butter Milkshake

Serves: 2

Prep Time: 5 minutes Cooking Time: 0 minutes

Ingredients:

1cup almond milk

1 whole banana, frozen 8 cherries, frozen

30 ml (2 tablespoons) almond butter

15 ml (1 tablespoon) honey Ice cubes, as many as you like

Directions:

1. Place all the ingredients into a food processor and blend until smooth and creamy. Serve and enjoy!

Nutritional Information (per serving)

Calories: 336

Fat total: 25.2g, saturated fat: 17.5G

Carbohydrates: 28.0g, dietary fiber: 3.3g Sugars: 13.2G, protein: 4.6g

32.
Ginger Brownies

Serves: 2

Prep Time: 5 minutes Cooking Time: 25 minutes

Ingredients:

500 ml (2 cups) almond flour 125 ml (½ cup) coconut flour

60 ml (4 tablespoons) cocoa powder, unsweetened

0.5 ml (⅛ teaspoon) cinnamon Pinch of salt

2 eggs

30 ml (2 tablespoons) coconut oil

30 ml (2 tablespoons) raw honey

15 ml (1 teaspoon) pure vanilla extract 1 teaspoon ground nutmeg

1 ml (¼ teaspoon) fresh ginger, minced

Directions:

1. Preheat the oven to 200°C/400°F. Lightly grease a baking pan.

2. Mix almond flour, coconut flour, cocoa powder, cinnamon, and salt in a bowl.

3. In another, bowl whisk the eggs.

4. Mix eggs with flour mixture and remaining ingredients.

5. Place into a baking pan.

6. Bake for 20-25 minutes until a toothpick inserted in the center comes out clean.

Nutritional Information (per serving)

Calories: 269

Fat total: 30.1G, saturated fat: 9.7g Carbohydrates: 20.2G, dietary fiber: 4.4 Sugars: 12.7G, protein: 7.2G

33.
Banana with Coconut & Almond Butter

Serves: 2

Prep Time: 10 minutes Cooking Time: 0 minutes

Ingredients:

1 banana, sliced

60 ml (4 tablespoons) coconut milk

60 ml (4 tablespoons) almond butter

0.5 ml (⅛ teaspoon) cinnamon

Directions:

1.   Toss all ingredients in a mixing bowl and sprinkle with cinnamon. Let it rest   5   minutes before serving in dessert bowls.

Nutritional Information (per serving)

Calories: 378

Fat total: 25.6g, saturated fat: 8.1G Carbohydrates: 34.4g, dietary fiber: 5.0g Sugars: 15.4g, protein: 8.8g

34.
Coconut Whipped Cream

Serves: 2

Prep Time: 5 minutes Refrigerating Time: 2-3 hours

Ingredients:

250 ml (1 cup) coconut cream

250 ml (1 cup) coconut milk 1 ml (¼ teaspoon) cinnamon

2.5 ml (½ teaspoon) vanilla extract 1 ml (¼ teaspoon) ground nutmeg

Directions:

1. Place all the ingredients in a food processor and blend until smooth and creamy.

2. Pour coconut cream in 4 cups, and refrigerate for at least 2 to 3 hours.

3. Serve and enjoy!

Nutritional Information (per serving)

Calories: 559

Fat total: 57.6g, saturated fat: 51.0G Carbohydrates: 14.0g, dietary fiber: 5.6g Sugars: 8.4g, protein: 5.6g

35.
Paleo Pumpkin Muffins

Serves: 5

Prep Time: 2 minutes Cooking Time: 25 minutes

Ingredients:

750 ml (1½ cup) almond flour

60 ml (4 tablespoons) coconut flour

5 ml (1 teaspoon) baking soda

5 ml (1 teaspoon) baking powder

2.5 ml (½ teaspoon) pumpkin pie spice

2.5 ml (½ teaspoon) ground cinnamon

0.5 ml (⅛ teaspoon) sea salt 2 large eggs

¾ cup pumpkin puree 60 ml (¼ cup) raw honey

30 ml (2 teaspoons) almond butter

15 ml (1 tablespoon) almonds, toasted and chopped

Directions:

1. Preheat the oven to 200°C/400°F.

2. Whisk almond flour, coconut flour, baking soda, baking powder, and pumpkin pie spice in a mixing bowl. Sprinkle with cinnamon and salt.

3. In another bowl, whisk the eggs. Add pumpkin puree, honey, and butter.

4. Mix wet ingredients with dry ingredients. Fill the batter in muffin cups until each is almost full.

5. Sprinkle with almonds.

6. Bake for 20 to 25 minutes or until a toothpick inserted in the center comes out clean.

Nutritional Information (per serving)

Calories: 189

Fat total: 8.7g, saturated fat: 1.4g Carbohydrates: 23.7, dietary fiber: 4.5g Sugars: 16.1G, protein: 6.3g

36.
Cauliflower Bites with Chili

Serves: 4

Prep Time: 10 minutes

Ingredients

1 large cauliflower head

2 tablespoons high heat oil 1/4 teaspoon salt

2 teaspoons of ancho chili powder

Directions:

1. Preheat your oven to 425°F (220°C or gas mark 7) and prepare a baking sheet with parchment paper.

2. Make the ancho chili pepper powder: Heat cast iron skillet on medium for a few minutes. Once hot, place the dried ancho chili in the skillet and shuffle for a few minutes, or until you begin to smell the aroma of it toasting. Then take it out and let cool. Remove the stem and seeds. Grind the remaining pepper in a coffee bean grinder, spice grinder, or food processor until it is has a powder consistency.

3. Chop the cauliflower into bite-size pieces.

4. Add the cauliflower pieces, ancho chili powder, salt, and oil to a large bowl and toss until the cauliflower is well coated.

5. After spreading the cauliflower across the baking sheet, bake for 30 minutes, or until the cauliflower bites are tender and a bit blackened.

6. Serve hot or very warm, with mint yogurt dip and slices of fresh lime.

7. Makes 4 appetizer or side dish servings

8. Includes 1/4 cup of your favorite homemade yogurt as a dip with a few mints leaves chopped up, a squeeze of lime, and a pinch or two of salt. Mix and serve.

Nutritional Information (per serving)

Calories: 170

Fat total: 15.7g, saturated fat: 3 g Carbohydrates: 15, dietary fiber: 6.5g Sugars: 16.1G, protein: 8g

37.
Almond Flour Waffles

Serves: 6

Prep Time: 12 minutes

Ingredients

1 cup of almond flour (or other nut flour)

1/4 teaspoon of salt

1/4 teaspoon of baking soda 4 eggs

1 teaspoon of vanilla

2 tablespoons of honey (or another sweetener)

1/4 teaspoon of cinnamon (optional) Orange Honey Syrup

½ cup of honey

¼ cup of fresh orange juice

1/8 teaspoon of vanilla extract (optional)

Blend all the ingredients together with a fork or whisk.

Directions:

1. Heat up your waffle iron.
2. Place the dry ingredients in a mixing bowl and blend with a whisk.

3. Add the wet ingredients to the dry ingredients. Blend all ingredients together.

4. Add 1/4 cup of the batter to your waffle iron and close the lid.

5. When the waffle is ready, take it out, place it on a plate. Next, add your favorite topping Seal left-over waffles and store in the refrigerator. Storage can range from refrigeration for a few days, or seal and freeze for a month makes about 6 waffles.

Nutritional Information (per serving)

Calories: 305

Fat total: 25g, Carbohydrates: 9g, dietary fiber: 5g Sugars: 3G, protein: 12g□

38.
Peanut Butter Cookies

Serves: 4

Prep Time: 5 minutes

Ingredients

¼ cup almond flour

1/2 cup raw clear honey [For 1 cup sugar which is not legal]

1 cup peanut butter

1 egg

½ teaspoon baking soda

2 tsp. Unsweetened coconut

Directions:

1. Mix all ingredients.
2. Roll into balls on a slip mat or cookie sheet.
3. Press with a fork.
4. Bake 8-10 minutes in an oven at 375 F.
5. Take out of the oven and sprinkle with coconut (unsweetened)

Nutritional Information (per serving)

Calories: 127

Fat total: 8g, Carbohydrates: 11g, dietary fiber: 1g
Sugars: 9g, protein: 4g☐

39.
SCD Beef Burritos

Serves: 2

Prep Time: 10 minutes

Beef Burritos

4 oz SCD yogurt

1 1/2 tsp ground cumin divided 1 1/2 ground turmeric divided

1 tablespoon olive oil, or coconut oil 1 lb. sirloin beef trips

1 medium white onion thinly sliced 4 carrots cut into matchsticks

1/2 lb. Nappa cabbage thinly sliced.

Tortilla's

Replace flour tortilla with egg crepe. SCD Crepes

1 large egg

2 TB cashew butter 2 TB apple cider

a dash of salt

1/8 tsp vanilla extract a pinch of cinnamon a pat of butter

Directions:

1. Beat eggs and mix in cashew butter and apple cider, salt, vanilla, and cinnamon.

2. Heat a small non-stick skillet and pour some of the crepe batter into the pan and swirl the pan to form the crepe.

3. Cook about 40 seconds. Flip and cook for another minute. Assemble burrito!

Nutritional Information (per serving)

Calories: 450

Fat total: 16g, Carbohydrates: 60g, dietary fiber: 6g
Sugars: 2.1g, protein: 22g☐

40.
Legal French Toast

Serves: 2

Prep Time: 7 minutes

Ingredients

Stale SCDiet Bread thick slices

2 eggs

1/2 cup sugar-free yogurt

1 tablespoon and 1/2 teaspoon clear raw honey

1 tablespoon vanilla, unsweetened

 1/2 teaspoon salt Whisk together

Directions:

1.   Dip sliced bread into the egg wash, Coat both sides

2.   Melt butter in a pan

3.   Cook till golden brown.

Nutritional Information (per serving)

Calories: 140

Fat total: 7g, Carbohydrates: 28g, dietary fiber: 1g
Sugars: 7.1g, protein: 5g☐

41.
Roasted Tomatoes

Serves: 4-6

Prep Time: 6 minutes

Ingredients

2-3lbs Roma Tomatoes cut in half

1 Glove Chopped Garlic

1 tsp Fresh Rosemary,

1 tsp Fresh Oregano

Pinch of salt and pepper to taste

2 tablespoons shredded parmesan cheese (optional)

2 tsp olive oil

Directions:

1. Preheat oven to 450°F.

2. Wash tomatoes and cut in half (if they're large tomatoes, cut into quarters).

3. Toss tomatoes with remaining ingredients. Place in a rimmed baking pan or dish. Roast 10-20 minutes or to desired doneness. Sprinkle with some parmesan cheese if desired.

Nutritional Information (per serving)

Calories: 114

Fat total: 6g, Carbohydrates: 12g, dietary fiber: 3g
Sugars: 8.1g, protein: 2.5g☐

42.
Specific Carbohydrate Diet Guacamole

Serves: 4-6

Prep Time: 10 minutes

Ingredients:

Cool Guacamole 4 ripe avocado

Juice of ½ lemon or lime 1 teaspoon salt

1/2 teaspoon ground cumin

1/2 teaspoon granulated garlic

1/4 teaspoon coriander

1/4 teaspoon pepper (or to taste)

1/4 teaspoon cayenne or chili powder (optional)

1 tablespoon chopped cilantro (optional)

1 medium tomato finely chopped (optional)

Directions:

1. Slice the avocado and place in a bowl.
2. Add the remaining ingredients and smash with a fork or spoon.
3. Mix well, but leave "chunky."
4. Yield: Serves 4 – 6

Nutritional Information (per serving)

Calories: 245

Fat total: 22g, Carbohydrates: 4g, dietary fiber: 2g
Sugars: 0g, protein: 3.5g☐

43.
Pulled Hawaiian Pork

Serves: 4

Prep Time: 10 minutes

Ingredients:

1 three lb. pork loin

1/2 cup Soy Sauce

1/2 cup apple cider

Fresh Thyme Herbs

1 Can Diced Pineapple

Directions:

1. Place meat in roasting pan and coat with all ingredients.

2. Cook the roast at 250*F. Oven for 5 hours or until pork pulls apart with a fork.

Nutritional Information (per serving)

Calories: 472

Fat total: 26g, Carbohydrates: 80g, dietary fiber: 0g
Sugars: 0g, protein: 35g☐

44.
Paleo Shrimp Scampi

Serves: 2

Prep Time: 10 minutes

Ingredients:

1Lb of shrimp

2.5 tsp olive oil

Garlic 2-3 cloves

Cherry tomatoes halved

1/2 cup SCD legal vegetable broth.

2-3 T butter

½ tsp Fresh oregano

½ tsp thyme

½ tarragon

Juice of lemon or lime

Directions:

1. In a pan on medium-high heat, add oil, melt butter, and ad juice of lemon or lime, herbs, and garlic.

2. Let cook 1-2 minutes then add shrimp.

3. Cook 3-4 minutes until shrimp or bright red.

4. Do not overcook.

Nutritional Information (per serving)

Calories: 417

Fat total: 9,5g, Carbohydrates: 45g, dietary fiber: 2.2g
Sugars: 2g, protein: 33g☐

45.
Eggs Baked in Avocado

Serves: 1

Prep Time: 10 minutes

Ingredients:

1 avocado

2 eggs

4-5 cherry tomatoes

1-2 garlic cloves, Fresh cilantro Salt and pepper

Directions:

1. Cut the avocado in half and scoop out more than the pit, just enough to hold a hardboiled egg.

2. Crack each egg into each avocado half and place it in a cookie sheet or baking dish.

3. Top with chopped tomatoes all seasoning and herbs

4. Bake for 20 minutes or until eggs are cooked.

Nutritional Information (per serving)

Calories: 230

Fat total: 19g, Carbohydrates: 9.5g, dietary fiber: 6.2g Sugars: 1g, protein: 7.5g☐

46.
Awesome Blossom Cauliflower

Serves: 4

Prep Time: 12 minutes

Ingredients:

1 large head of Cauliflower cut into pieces

6-8 strips of bacon cooked and chopped or pancetta cubed

6 tablespoons chopped chives and fresh dill

2 cups Colby Jack Cheese (or Romano)

2-3T olive oil

Directions:

1. Place Cauliflower on a baking sheet and drizzle with olive oil spices herbs and cheese.

2. Bake for 15-20 minutes @ 425 Degrees until cheese is melted.

3. Top with remaining 3 T chives and serve.

Nutritional Information (per serving)

Calories: 129

Fat total: 9g, Carbohydrates: 8.5g, dietary fiber: 2.2g
Sugars: 2g, protein: 4g☐

47.
Banana Muffins

Serves: 4-6

Prep Time: 12 minutes

Ingredients:

4 medium eggs, room temperature

3 tablespoons clear raw honey

1 teaspoon vanilla, unsweetened

2 tablespoons coconut oil softened

½ teaspoon apple cider vinegar

½ cup coconut flour, unsweetened

¼ cup blanched almond flour

½ teaspoon ground cinnamon 1 teaspoon baking soda

½ teaspoon salt

1 overly ripe medium-sized bananas

¼ cup milk/coconut milk/almond milk

¼ cup chocolate chips (optional)*

Directions:

1. Mix all ingredients in a mixing bowl and spoon into greased muffin tin.

2. Bake 350 degrees for 18-24 minutes until golden brown

Nutritional Information (per serving)

Calories: 210

Fat total: 13g, Carbohydrates: 19g, dietary fiber: 4g
Sugars: 10g, protein: 5g□

48.
Bacon-Wrapped Steak with Onions and Mushrooms

Serves: 2

Prep Time: 15 minutes

Ingredients:

2 fillet mignon medallions

8 oz whole mushrooms, sliced in half 1 medium onion, sliced

8-10 slices bacon

2 tbs olive oil

1 tsp salt

1/2 tsp pepper

Directions:

1. Wrap bacon around fillets, season with salt and pepper, and place on a BBQ grill.

2. Sauté onions and mushrooms pour over steak.

Nutritional Information (per serving)

Calories: 386

Fat total: 14g, Carbohydrates: 13g, dietary fiber: 1g
Sugars: 2g, protein: 31g☐

49.
Calming Coconut Smoothie

Servings: 1

Prep Time: 3 minutes

Ingredients:

1 cups pineapple

1 tablespoon coconut oil

 1 cup kale

1 pinch of cinnamon

Directions:

Prepare ingredients and place into a blender. Blend together while adding preferred liquid until desired consistency is reached.

Nutritional Info Per Serving:

Calories 105 Carbs 12 g Fat 5 g

Protein 1 g

50.
Anti-Inflammatory Smoothie

Servings: 2-3

Prep Time: 3 minutes

Ingredients:

1 cups beets

½ cup almonds 2 oranges

Pinch of turmeric

Directions:

Prepare ingredients and place into a blender. Blend together while adding preferred liquid until desired consistency is reached.

Nutritional Info Per Serving:

Calories 199, Carbs 29 g, Fat 9 g,

 Protein 6 g

51.
Berry Anti-Inflammatory Smoothie

Servings: 2

Prep Time: 3 minutes

Ingredients:

2 cups of beets

½ of crushed almonds 3 cups strawberries Dash of turmeric

Directions:

Prepare ingredients and place into a blender. Blend together while adding preferred liquid until desired consistency is reached.

Nutritional Info Per Serving:

Calories 97, Carbs 23 g, Fat 1 g,

Protein 2 g

52.
Beets'n'Nuts Smoothie

Servings: 2-3

Prep Time: 3 minutes

Ingredients:

2 cups beets

½ cup crushed almonds 3 mangos

Dash of paprika

Directions:

Prepare ingredients and place into a blender. Blend together while adding preferred liquid until desired consistency is reached.

Nutritional Info Per Serving:

Calories 212, Carbs 32 g, Fat 8 g, Protein

6 g

53.
Cauliflangonut Smoothie

Servings: 2-3

Prep Time: 3 minutes

Ingredients:

2 cups of beets

1 cup cauliflower

3 mangos

1 tablespoon coconut oil

Directions:

Prepare ingredients and place into a blender. Blend together while adding preferred liquid until desired consistency is reached.

Nutritional Info Per Serving:

Calories 167, Carbs 30 g, Fat 5 g, Protein

3 g

54.
Red and White Smoothie

Servings: 2-3

Prep Time: 3 minutes

Ingredients:

2 cups beets

1 cup cauliflower

3 cups strawberries

2 tablespoon coconut oil

Directions:

Prepare ingredients and place into a blender. Blend together while adding preferred liquid until desired consistency is reached.

Nutritional Info Per Serving:

Calories 182, Carbs 24 g, Fat 10 g,

Protein 4 g

55.
Cauliflower Power Smoothie

Servings: 2-3

Prep Time: 3 minutes

Ingredients:

2 cups beets

1 cup cauliflower

3 oranges

1 tablespoon coconut oil

Directions:

Prepare ingredients and place into a blender. Blend together while adding preferred liquid until desired consistency is reached.

Nutritional Info Per Serving:

Calories 184, Carbs 35 g, Fat 5 g, Protein

4 g

Paleo Smoothies for Post-workout Support

If you are curious about the purpose of post-workout smoothies, they are designed to maximize the potential muscle gain of all that laborious exercise. Without the proper diet and nutritional content, you will see very few results from your workouts. If you genuinely want to build muscle and burn fat, you must consume the right foods after your workouts.

Add crushed ice or whatever your favorite liquid is and enjoy it. Makes 2-3 servings per recipe.

56.
Grapes of Watermelon Smoothie

Servings: *2-3*

Prep Time: 3 minutes

Ingredients:

2 cups watermelon

1 cup grapes

1 banana

Directions:

Prepare ingredients and place into a blender. Blend together while adding preferred liquid until desired consistency is reached.

Nutritional Info Per Serving:

Calories 86, Carbs 22 g, Fat 0 g, Protein

1 g

57.
Blueberry Pear Smoothie

Servings: 2-3

Prep Time: 3 minutes

Ingredients:

1 cups watermelon

2 pears

2 cups blueberries

Directions:

Prepare ingredients and place into a blender. Blend together while adding preferred liquid until desired consistency is reached.

Nutritional Info Per Serving:

Calories 166, Carbs 43 g, Fat 1 g, Protein

2 g

58.
RePEARer Smoothie

Servings: *2-3*

Prep Time: 3 minutes

Ingredients:

2 cups watermelon

2 bananas

Dash of turmeric

Dash of cinnamon

2 pears

Directions:

Prepare ingredients and place into a blender. Blend together while adding preferred liquid until desired consistency is reached.

Nutritional Info Per Serving:

Calories 182, Carbs 47 g, Fat 0 g, Protein 2g

59.
Asparagus Smoothie

Servings: *2-3*

Prep Time: 3 minutes

Ingredients:

2 pears

2 cups grapes

1 cup asparagus (trimmed)

Directions:

Prepare ingredients and place into a blender. Blend together while adding preferred liquid until desired consistency is reached.

Nutritional Info Per Serving:

Calories 171, Carbs 45 g, Fat 1 g, Protein

1 g

60.
Blueberry Smoothie

Servings: *2-3*

Prep Time: 3 minutes

Ingredients:

2 pears

2 cups blueberries

1 cup asparagus (trimmed)

Directions:

Prepare ingredients and place into a blender. Blend together while adding preferred liquid until desired consistency is reached.

Nutritional Info Per Serving:

Calories 145,

Carbs 38 g,

Fat 1 g

Protein 2 g

Conclusion

I hope this book has given you some new ideas for smoothies and that you have found some favorites. As you have learned, the human body evolved to naturally digest fruits, vegetables, meats, and fish over thousands of years. And finally, there is a diet that can indeed supply the human body with what it was meant to ingest.

The next step is to make the smoothies included in this book, utilizing them to fuel your muscle building, toning, retention, recovery, pre-workout, and post-workout efforts. Take what you love about them and keep it. If you hated the recipe, try taking out one ingredient and adding in another. I know not every smoothie will be to your liking, but that is what makes smoothies great. There is so much flexibility.

These are the weight loss shakes needed for the protection and support of our lean muscle tissue. If you ever wondered why your slim friend could eat whatever they want and never gain weight, it is their muscle tissue at work for them.

Drink up, lean up, and burn fat all day long.

Please feel free to look into the author's other books related to curing Ulcerative Colitis and Crohn's disease that works in conjunction with these recipes

How To Cure Ulcerative Colitis In 90 Days: Alternative Non-Toxic Treatment That Works Kindle Edition

https://www.amazon.com/dp/B06VTKPTKV

How To Cure Crohn's Disease in 90 Days: Alternative Healthy Treatment That Works Kindle Edition

https://www.amazon.com/dp/B06XKNC3NT

Ulcerative Colitis & Crohn's Disease Cookbook Specific Carbohydrate Diet & Paleo Cookbook:

https://www.amazon.com/dp/B073Z37QM3

Made in the USA
Monee, IL
05 October 2023

44019544R00076